WOOD PELLET SMOKER AND GRILL COOKBOOK

The Ultimate Guide for Perfect
Sauces and Snacks

Linda Eleanor Geary

Table of contents:

Additionally, the information in the following pages is intended only for informational purposes and should thus be thought of as universal. As befitting its nature, it is presented without assurance regarding its prolonged validity or interim quality. Trademarks that are mentioned are done without written consent and can in no way be considered an endorsement from the trademark holder.

INTRODUCTION

Pellet grills, also known as pellet smokers, are outdoor cooking units that combine the characteristics of charcoal smokers, gas grills and conventional ovens. Using wood pellets as combustion power they can grill, sear and bake with the help of an electronic panel that supplies the fire with pellets while adjusting the air flow inside the grill and maintaining an optimum temperature.

A wood pellet is shaped like a pill that looks like a quarter-inch thick wood. Wood pellets are available in different varieties, like hickory, apple, mesquite, cherry and more. Different varieties provide different tastes and levels of smokiness for prepared food.

Wood pellets are discarded in a container called a hopper. The pellets then move within the grid using an electrically powered auger. Wood pellets ignite easily, producing heat and cooking while adding wood flavor.

Preheat usually takes about 15 minutes. This makes cooking effective and easy for anyone. You can choose anytime and work out some delicious recipes.

As in an oven, the grates burn at a precise temperature depending on how many of them are fed by the auger. The number of pellets directly affects the temperature of the pellet grids.

The most important thing you need to keep in mind when exchanging your old grade for a pellet griddle smoker is versatility. You will be able to perfectly cook a wider range of meats, cuts and vegetables.

In different degrees, with different flavors based on the wood pellets you choose. The choices are limitless and only your creativity will limit you.

SAUCES AND SNACKS

1. Bacon Dressing Romaine Salad

Preparation time: 10 minutes Cooking Time: 2 minutes Total time: 12 minutes Servings: 2-4

Pellet: Alder

Ingredients:

- 1 Lettuce heart

- 2 tbsp. grated Parmesan
- 1 tbsp. of Olive oil
- Black pepper and salt to taste
- Bacon dressing:
- 6 slices of Bacon, cook and then crumbled
- ½ Tsp. Garlic powder
- Black pepper and salt to taste
- ¼ cup of milk
- 2 tbsp. Mayo
- 2 tbsp. of Bleu Cheese

Directions:

1. Preheat the grill to 450F with closed lid.
2. The lettuce hearts in half. Brush with oil. Season with black pepper and salt to taste. Sprinkle Parmesan cheese.
3. Grill for 2 minutes.
4. Make the dressing. In a bowl combine the mayo, bleu cheese, and milk. Season with black pepper, garlic powder, and salt. Add the crumbled bacon.
5. Assemble: add the dressing on top of the lettuce. If you like you can add more cheese.
6. Serve and enjoy!

Nutrition: Calories: 165 Protein: 10g Carbs: 2g Fat: 8g

2. Bacon BBQ Bites

Preparation time: 10 minutes Cooking Time: 25 minutes Total time: 35 minutes Servings: 2-4

Pellet: Hickory

Ingredients:

- 1 tbsp. Fennel, ground
- ½ cup of Brown Sugar
- 1 lb. Slab Bacon, cut into cubes (1 inch)
- 1 tsp. Black pepper
- Salt

Directions:

1. Take an aluminum foil and then fold in half. Once you do that, then turn the edges so that a rim is made. With a fork make small holes on the bottom. In this way, the excess fat will escape and will make the bites crispy.
2. Preheat the grill to 350F with closed lid.
3. In a bowl combine the black pepper, salt, fennel, and sugar. Stir.
4. Place the pork in the seasoning mixture. Toss to coat. Transfer on the foil.
5. Place the foil on the grill. Bake for 25 minutes, or until crispy and bubbly.
6. Serve and enjoy!

Nutrition: Calories: 300 Protein: 27g Carbs: 4g Fat: 36g

3. Baked Wings with Parmesan and Garlic

Preparation time: 10 minutes Cooking Time: 30 minutes Total time: 40 minutes Servings: 4-6

Pellet: Cherry

Ingredients:

- ½ cup Poultry seasoning rub
- 5 lbs. of Chicken Wings

Sauce:

- 2 tbsp. Poultry Seasoning Rub
- 10 Garlic cloves, diced
- 1 cup unsalted Butter

For garnish:

- 3 tbsp. chopped Parsley
- 1 cup shredded Parmesan cheese

Directions:

1. Preheat the grill with the lid closed to high.
2. In a bowl place the wings and add the seasoning rub. Toss well to coat. Cook directly on the grate for 10 min. Then flip and cook for 10 more minutes. The internal temperature must be 165F to 180 F.
3. In the meantime, make the sauce, combine the garlic and butter in a saucepan and cook over medium for about 10 minutes. Stir occasionally.
4. When the wings are done transfer into a bowl. Toss with the sauce, parsley, and Parmesan cheese. Serve and enjoy!

Nutrition: Calories: 310 Proteins: 19g Carbs: 2g Fat: 14g

4. Bean Salad

Preparation time: 10 minutes Cooking Time: 30 minutes Total time: 40 minutes Servings: 6-8

Pellet: Oak

Ingredients:

- 1 can of Kidney Beans, rinsed and drained
- 1 can of Northern beans, rinsed and drained
- ½ tbsp. Oil
- 1lb. of Green beans, trim the ends

- 1 shaved Shallot
- 1 Garlic clove, minced
- 2 tbsp. Wine vinegar, red
- 1 tbsp. Parsley, chopped
- 1 tsp. of Dijon mustard
- ¼ cup oil
- Black pepper and salt to taste

Directions:

1. Preheat the grill to smoke and close the lid.
2. Spread the beans on a baking tray. Place on the grate. Smoke for 20 minutes. Set aside.
3. Increase the temperature 450F and close the lid.
4. Season the green and drizzle with ½ tbsp. oil. Spread directly on the grate. Cook 10 minutes. Set aside to cool.
5. In the meantime, make the salad dressing. In a bowl combine the mustard, vinegar, garlic, and shallot. Whisk. Add olive oil and whisk again. Season with black pepper and salt and add parsley. Stir to combine.
6. In a bowl combine the beans. Drizzle with the salad dressing. Adjust seasoning and serve in a dish.
7. Garnish with parsley and serve. Enjoy!

Nutrition: Calories: 180 Protein: 9g Carbs: 26g Fat: 5g

5. Broccoli Onion Salad

Preparation time: 5 minutes Cooking Time: 15 minutes Total time: 20 minutes Servings: 6-8

Pellet: Alder

Ingredients:

- 1 Onion halved (red)
- 2 Broccoli heads, broken into florets
- 1 cup halved cherry Tomatoes

- 4 tbsp. Olive oil
- 2 ½ tbsp. of Rice Vinegar
- Black pepper and salt to taste
- 2 tbsp. chopped Parsley

Directions:

1. Preheat the grill to 450F with closed lid.
2. In a bowl add the broccoli. Season with black pepper of salt and drizzle with 2 tbsp. olive oil. Toss to combine. Place the florets on a sheet pan lined with foil. Grill until charred. Make sure to toss occasionally.
3. Brush the onion with oil. Grill until charred. Remove from the grill and slice into pieces (1/4 inch).
4. In a bowl add the tomatoes, drizzle with rice vinegar and oil. Add the onions and season with black pepper and salt to taste. Toss again.
5. Place the florets on a plate and add the mixture evenly over them.
6. Garnish with chopped parsley. Serve and enjoy!

Nutrition: Calories: 220 Protein: 5g Carbs: 18g Fat: 10g

6. Cinnamon Almonds

Preparation time: 10 minutes Cooking Time: 1 hour and 30 minutes Total time: 1 hour and 40 minutes Servings: 4-6

Pellet: Hickory

Ingredients:

- 1 egg, the white
- 1lb. Almonds
- ½ cup of Brown Sugar
- ½ cup of Granulated sugar
- 1/8 tsp. Salt
- 1 tbsp. ground Cinnamon

Directions:

1. Whisk the egg white until frothy. Add the salt, cinnamon, and sugars. Add the almonds and toss to coat.
2. Spread the almonds on a baking dish lined with parchment paper. Make sure they are in a single layer.
3. Preheat the grill to 225F with closed lid.
4. Grill for 1 h and 30 minutes. Stir often.
5. Serve slightly cooled and enjoy!

Nutrition: Calories: 280 Protein: 10g Carbs: 38g Fat: 13g

7. Corn Salsa

Preparation time: 10 minutes Cooking Time: 15 minutes Total time: 25 minutes Servings: 4

Pellet: Mesquite

Ingredients:

- 4 Ears Corn, large with the husk on
- 4 Tomatoes (Roma) diced and seeded
- 1 tsp. of Onion powder

- 1 tsp. of Garlic powder
- 1 Onion, diced
- ½ cup chopped Cilantro
- Black pepper and salt to taste
- 1 lime, the juice
- 1 grille jalapeno, diced

Directions:

1. Preheat the grill to 450F.
2. Place the ears corn on the grate and cook until charred. Remove husk. Cut into kernels.
3. Combine all ingredients, plus the corn and mix well. Refrigerate before serving.
4. Enjoy!

Nutrition: Calories: 120 Protein: 2f Carbs: 4g Fat: 1g

8. Creamy Egg Salad

Preparation time: 20 minutes Cooking Time: 30 minutes Total time: 50 minutes Servings: 4-6

Pellet: Oak

Ingredients:

- ¾ cup Mayo
- 2 tbsp. green onion or chives, minced
- 1 Stalk of celery, diced finely
- 12 Eggs, large, hard - boiled and peeled

- 2 tsp. of Mustard
- 2 tsp. Lemon juice, fresh
- Black pepper and salt to taste
- Crackers or bread
- For garnish: smoked paprika

Directions:

1. Preheat the grill to smoke, close the lid.
2. Place the eggs on the grate. Smoke for about 30 minutes. Set aside to cool.
3. Once cooled dice the smoked eggs and transfer in a bowl. Add the mustard, lemon juice, mayo, chives, and celery. Season with black pepper and salt to taste.
4. Serve in smaller salad serving bowls. Dust with smoked paprika.
5. Serve with crackers or bread.
6. Enjoy!

Nutrition: Calories: 180 Protein: 5g Carbs: 2g Fat: 8g

9. Devilled Eggs

Preparation time: 15 minutes Cooking Time: 30 minutes Total time: 45 minutes Servings: 4-6

Pellet: Hickory

Ingredients:

- 3 tsp. diced chives
- 3 tbsp. Mayo
- 7 Eggs, hard - boiled, peeled
- 1 tsp. Cider vinegar

- 1 tsp. Mustard, brown
- 1/8 tsp. Hot sauce
- 2 tbsp. crumbled Bacon
- Black pepper and salt to taste
- For dusting: Paprika

Directions:

1. Preheat the grill to 180F with closed lid.
2. Place the cooked eggs on the grate. Smoke 30 minutes. Set aside and let them cool.
3. Slice the eggs in half lengthwise. Scoop the yolks and transfer into a ziplock bag. Now add the black pepper, salt, hot sauce, vinegar, mustard, chives, and mayo. Close the bag and knead the ingredients until smooth.
4. Cut one corner and squeeze the mixture into the egg whites.
5. Top with bacon and dust with paprika.
6. Serve and enjoy!
7. Or chill in the fridge until serving.

Nutrition: Calories: 140 Protein: 6g Carbs: 2g Fat: 6g

10.   Grilled French Dip

Preparation time: 15 minutes Cooking Time: 35 minutes Total time: 50 minutes Servings: 8-12

Pellet: Mesquite

Ingredients:

- 3 lbs. onions, thinly sliced (yellow)
- 2 tbsp. oil
- 2 tbsp. of Butter
- Salt to taste
- Black pepper to taste

- 1 tsp. Thyme, chopped
- 2 tsp. of Lemon juice
- 1 cup Mayo
- 1 cup of Sour cream

Directions:

1. Preheat the grill to high with closed lid.
2. In a pan combine the oil and butter. Place on the grill to melt. Add 2 tsp. salt and add the onions.
3. Stir well and close the lid of the grill. Cook 30 minutes stirring often.
4. Add the thyme. Cook for an additional 3 minutes. Set aside and add black pepper.
5. Once cooled add lemon juice, mayo, and sour cream. Stir to combine. Taste and add more black pepper and salt if needed.
6. Serve with veggies or chips.
7. Enjoy!

Nutrition: Calories: 60 Protein: 4g Carbs: 5g Fat: 6g

11.   Grilled Watermelon

Preparation time: 10 minutes Cooking Time: 15 minutes Total time: 25 minutes Servings: 4

Pellet: Apple

Ingredients:

- 2 Limes
- 2 tbsp. oil
- ½ Watermelon, sliced into wedges
- ¼ Tsp. Pepper flakes
- 2 tbsp. Salt

Directions:

1. Preheat the grill to high with closed lid.
2. Brush the watermelon with oil. Grill for 15 minutes. Flip once.
3. In a blender mix the salt and pepper flakes until combined.
4. Transfer the watermelon on a plate. Drizzle with lime juice and sprinkle with the seasoning mixture you made.
5. Serve and enjoy!

Nutrition: Calories: 40 Protein: 1g Carbs: 10g Fat: 0

12.   Jalapeno Poppers

Preparation time: 15 minutes Cooking Time: 1-hour Total time: 1 hour and 15 minutes Servings: 4-6

Pellet: Mesquite

Ingredients:

- 6 Bacon slices halved
- 12 Jalapenos, medium
- 1 cup grated Cheese
- 8 oz. softened Cream cheese
- 2 tbsp. Poultry seasoning

29

Directions:

1. Preheat the grill to 180F with closed lid.
2. Cut the jalapenos lengthwise. Clean them from the ribs and seeds.
3. Mix the poultry seasoning, grated cheese, and cream cheese.
4. Fill each jalapeno with the mixture and wrap with 1 half bacon. Place a toothpick to secure it. Place them on a baking sheet and smoke and grill 20 minutes.
5. Increase the temperature of the grill to 375F. Cook for 30 minutes more.
6. Serve and enjoy!

Nutrition: Calories: 60 Protein: 4g Carbs: 2g Fat: 8g

13.   Nut Mix on the Grill

Preparation time: 15 minutes Cooking Time: 20 minutes Total time: 35 minutes Servings: 8

Pellet: Oak

Ingredients:

- 3 cups Mixed Nuts, salted
- 1 tsp. Thyme, dried
- 1 ½ tbsp. brown sugar, packed
- 1 tbsp. Olive oil
- ¼ tsp. of Mustard powder
- ¼ tsp. Cayenne pepper

Directions:

1. Preheat the grill to 250F with closed lid.
2. In a bowl combine the ingredients and place the nuts on a baking tray lined with parchment paper. Place the try on the grill. Cook 20 minutes.
3. Serve and enjoy!

Nutrition: Calories: 65 Protein: 23g Carbs 4g: Fat: 52g

14. Onion Bacon Ring

Preparation time: 10 minutes Cooking Time: 1 hour and 30 minutes Total time: 1 hour and 40 minutes Servings: 6-8

Pellet: Mesquite

Ingredients:

- 2 large Onions, cut into ½ inch slices
- 1 Package of Bacon
- 1 tsp. of Honey
- 1 tbsp. Mustard, yellow
- 1 tbsp. Garlic chili sauce

Directions:

1. Wrap Bacon around onion rings. Wrap until you out of bacon. Place on skewers.
2. Preheat the grill to 400F with closed lid.
3. In the meantime, on a bowl combine the mustard and garlic chili sauce. Add honey and stir well.
4. Grill the onion bacon rings for 1 h and 30 minutes. Flip once.
5. Serve with the sauce and enjoy!

Nutrition: Calories: 90 Protein: 2g Carbs: 9g Fat: 7g

15.   Peppercorn Steaks & Creamy Sauce

Preparation time: 1 hour and 20 minutes Cooking Time: 1 hour and 30 minutes Total time: 2 hours and 50 minutes Servings: 4-6

Pellet: Hickory

Ingredients:

For the Steaks:

- 4 Beef Tenderloin Steaks
- Coarsely ground black pepper

- Coarsely ground green peppercorns
- Salt to taste
- 2 tbsp. Cold coffee (strong) or Bourbon
- 2 Garlic cloves, minced
- ½ cup of Dijon Mustard
- 1 tbsp. Worcestershire sauce

Creamy Sauce:

- ½ cup of Heavy cream
- ½ cup of Chicken Stock
- ½ cup Wine, white
- 1 Garlic clove, minced
- 16 oz. Mushrooms, thinly sliced (Crimini)
- 1 tbsp. Oil

Directions:

1. In a bowl add the Worcestershire sauce, bourbon or coffee, garlic, and mustard. Whisk well to combine.
2. Lay the tenderloin steaks on a plastic wrap and spread the mixture over the meat. Wrap the tenderloin tightly. Let it sit for about 1 hour at room temperature.
3. Unwrap and season with green peppercorns, black pepper, and salt. Pat the seasoning onto the steak. Preheat the grill to 180F with the lid closed.

4. Place the steaks on the grate. Smoke for 1 hour. Set aside.

5. Set the temperature of the grill to high. Close the grill. Once hot cook the steaks for 2 - 30 minutes or until the internal temperature is 130F.

6. Make the creamy sauce. Add the onions after heating the oil in pan and Sauté for few minutes and then add the garlic. Pour the stock and wine and add the mushrooms. Let it simmer for 7 minutes, or until the sauce is thickened. Season with black pepper and salt to taste. Set aside.

7. Transfer the steaks on a plate and let it rest for about 10 minutes (covered with foil). Carve into slices.

8. Serve the steaks topped with sauce and enjoy!

Nutrition: Calories: 250 Proteins: 38g Carbs: 4g Fat: 20g

16.   Roasted Cashews

Preparation time: 15 minutes Cooking Time: 12 minutes Total time: 27 minutes Servings: 6

Pellet: Oak

Ingredients:

- ¼ cup Rosemary, chopped
- 2 ½ tbsp. Butter, melted
- 2 cups Cashews, raw
- ½ tsp. of Cayenne pepper
- 1 tsp. of salt

Directions:

1. Preheat the grill to 350F with closed lid.
2. In a baking dish lay the nuts. Combine the cayenne, salt rosemary, and butter. Add on top. Toss to combine.
3. Grill for 12 minutes.
4. Serve and enjoy!

Nutrition: Calories: 150 Proteins: 5g Carbs: 7g Fat: 15g

17.Shrimp Cocktail

Preparation time: 10 minutes Cooking Time: 10 minutes Total time: 20 minutes Servings: 2-4

Pellet: Mesquite

Ingredients:

- 2 lbs. of Shrimp with tails, deveined
- Black pepper and salt
- 1 tsp. of Old Bay

- 2 tbsp. Oil
- ½ cup of Ketchup
- 1 tbsp. of Lemon Juice
- 2 tbsp. Horseradish, Prep Timeared
- 1 tbsp. of Lemon juice
- For garnish: chopped parsley
- Optional: Hot sauce

Directions:

1. Preheat the grill to 350F with closed lid.
2. Clean the shrimp. Pat dry using paper towels.
3. In a bowl add the shrimp, Old Bay, and oil. Toss to coat. Spread on a baking tray. Place the tray on the grill and let it cook for 7 minutes.
4. In the meantime, make the sauce: Combine the lemon juice, horseradish, and ketchup. Season with black pepper and sauce and if you like add hot sauce. Stir.
5. Serve the shrimp with the sauce and enjoy!

Nutrition: Calories: 80 Protein: 8g Carbs: 5g Fat: 1g

18.   Roasted Tomatoes

Preparation time: 10 minutes Cooking Time: 3 hours Total time: 3 hours and 10 minutes

Servings: 2-4

Pellet: Alder

Ingredients:

- 3 ripe Tomatoes, large
- 1 tbsp. black pepper
- 2 tbsp. Salt

- 2 tsp. Basil
- 2 tsp. of Sugar
- Oil

Directions:

1. Place a parchment paper on a baking sheet. Preheat the grill to 225F with closed lid.
2. Remove the stems from the tomatoes. Cut them into slices (1/2 inch).
3. In a bowl combine the basil, sugar, pepper, and salt. Mix well.
4. Pour oil on a plate. Dip the tomatoes (just one side) in the oil. Transfer on the Prep Timeared baking sheet.
5. Dust each slice with the mixture.
6. Grill the tomatoes for 3 hours.
7. Serve and enjoy! (You can serve it with mozzarella pieces).

Nutrition: Calories: 40 Protein: 1g Carbs: 2g Fat: 3g

19. Smoked Burger with Cheese Sauce

Preparation time: 15 minutes Cooking Time: 1-hour Total time: 1 hour and 15 minutes

Servings: 4-6

Pellet: Hickory

Ingredients:

For the sauce:

- ¼ cup of Milk
- 1 tsp. Red hot sauce
- 1 tbsp. of Butter
- 2 Garlic cloves, minced
- 16 oz. Cheese, Velveeta

Burgers:

- 4 Burger Buns
- 3 tsp. Beef Rub
- 2 lbs. Beef, ground
- 1 lb. Green chilies, grilled, pilled and sliced into strips
- 2 Garlic cloves, minced
- ½ Onion, sliced
- 1 tbsp. unsalted Butter

Directions:

1. Preheat the grill to 180F.
2. Make the sauce. In a pan that is oven safe heat the butter. Add the garlic. Sauté for 30 seconds and then add the cheese. Stir and cook until melted. Add the hot sauce.
3. Transfer on the grill. Smoke for about 30 minutes. Set aside.
4. Make the chili - onions: In a pan heat butter. Cook the onions until tender. Add garlic and chills. Cook until warmed. Set aside.
5. Increase the temperature to 500F (if you have 500F).
6. Now form 4 patties from the beef. Season with the Beef Rub.
7. Cook the burgers for 10 minutes per side. Flip them after the first 5 minutes.
8. Cut the buns and grill them for 3 minutes.
9. Assemble the burgers. Place the patty first on the bun pour the sauce and add the chili onion.
10. Serve and enjoy!

Nutrition: Calories: 620 Proteins: 30g Carbs: 55g Fat: 30g

20.   Smoked Guacamole

Preparation time: 25 minutes Cooking Time: 30 minutes Total time: 55 minutes

Servings: 6-8

Pellet: Apple

Ingredients:

- ¼ cup chopped Cilantro
- 7 Avocados, peeled and seeded
- ¼ cup chopped Onion, red
- ¼ cup chopped tomato
- 3 ears corn
- 1 tsp. of Chile Powder
- 1 tsp. of Cumin
- 2 tbsp. of Lime juice
- 1 tbsp. minced Garlic
- 1 Chile, poblano
- Black pepper and salt to taste

Directions:

1. Preheat the grill to 180F with closed lid.
2. Smoke the avocado for 10 min.
3. Set the avocados aside and increase the temperature of the girl to high.
4. Once heated grill the corn and chili. Roast for 20 minutes.
5. Cut the corn. Set aside. Place the chili in a bowl. Cover with a plastic wrap and let it sit for about 10 minutes. Peel the chili and dice. Add it to the kernels.
6. In a bowl mash the avocados, leave few chunks. Add the remaining ingredients and mix.
7. Serve right away because it is best eaten fresh. Enjoy!

Nutrition: Calories: 51 Protein: 1g Carbs: 3g Fat: 4.5g

21.   Smoked Jerky

Preparation time: 20 minutes Cooking Time: 6 hours Total time: 6 hours and 20 minutes

Servings: 6-8

Pellet: Oak

Ingredients:

- 1 Flank Steak (3lb.)
- ½ cup of Brown Sugar
- 1 cup of Bourbon
- ¼ cup Jerky rub

- 2 tbsp. of Worcestershire sauce
- 1 can of Chioplete
- ½ cup Cider Vinegar

Directions:

1. Slice the steak into ¼ inch slices.
2. Combine the remaining ingredients in a bowl. Stir well.
3. Place the steak in a plastic bag and add the marinade sauce. Marinade in the fridge overnight.
4. Preheat the grill to 180F with closed lid.
5. Remove the flank from marinade. Place directly on a rack and on the grill.
6. Smoke for 6 hours.
7. Cover them lightly for 1 hour before serving. Store leftovers in the fridge.

Nutrition: Calories: 105 Protein: 14g Carbs 4g: Fat: 3g

22. Smoked Mushrooms

Preparation time: 5 minutes Cooking Time: 45 minutes Total time: 50 minutes Servings: 4-6

Pellet: Apple

Ingredients:

- 4 cups Mushrooms (whole) baby Portobello, cleaned
- 1 tsp. of Onion powder
- 1 tbsp. of Canola Oil
- 1 tsp. garlic, granulated
- 1 tsp. of Pepper
- 1 tsp. of Salt

Directions:

1. Add the ingredients in a bowl. Toss to combine.
2. Preheat the grill to smoke with closed lid.
3. Smoke the mushrooms for about 30 minutes. Before finishing increase the heat and cook 15 minutes more.
4. Serve and enjoy!

Nutrition: Calories: 55 Protein: 2.5g Carbs: 3g Fat: 3.5g

23.Smoked Popcorn with Parmesan Herb

Preparation time: 10 minutes Cooking Time: 10 minutes Total time: 20 minutes

Servings: 2-4

Pellet: Cherry

Ingredients:

- ¼ cup of Popcorn Kernels
- 1 tsp. of salt

- 1 tsp. of Garlic powder
- ½ cup grated Parmesan
- 2 tsp. of Italian seasoning
- 2 tbsp. oil
- 4 tbsp. of Butter

Directions:

1. Preheat the grill to 250F with closed lid.
2. In a saucepan add the butter and oil. Melt and add the salt, garlic powder, and Italian seasoning. Set aside.
3. Add the kernels in a paper bag. Fold it two times to close.
4. Place in the microwave. Turn on high heat and set 2 minutes.
5. Open and transfer into a bowl.
6. Pour the butter. Toss. Transfer on a baking tray and grill for about 10 minutes. 2 minutes before the end sprinkle with Parmesan cheese.
7. Serve and enjoy!

Nutrition: Calories: 60 Protein: 1g Carbs: 5g Fat: 3g

24.   Smoked Summer Sausage

Preparation time: 15 minutes Cooking Time: 4 hours Total time: 4 hours and 15 minutes Servings: 4-6

Pellet: Apple

Ingredients:

- 1 ½ tsp. of Morton Salt
- ½ lb. Ground venison
- ½ lb. of ground Boar

- 1 tbsp. Salt
- ½ tsp. of mustard seeds
- ½ tsp. of Garlic powder
- ½ tsp. of Black pepper

Directions:

1. Add all ingredients into a bowl and mix until combined. Cover the bowl with a plastic bag and let it rest in the fridge overnight
2. Form a log from the mixture and wrap with a plastic wrap. Twist the log's end tightly. Now unwrap carefully.
3. Preheat the grill to 225F with closed lit.
4. Grill the meat for 4 hours. Set aside and let it cool for 1 hour.
5. Once cooled wrap and store in the fridge.
6. Serve and enjoy!

Nutrition: Calories: 170 Protein: 8g Carbs: 0 Fat: 14g

25.   Spicy Shrimp

Preparation time: 10 minutes Cooking Time: 6 minutes Servings: 6

Pellet: Apple

Ingredients:

- 24 shrimp (2 lbs.) deveined and peeled
- 3 tbsp. oil

- 1 Onion, diced
- 2 Garlic cloves, minced
- ½ Jalapeno pepper, minced
- 1 cup Spicy BBQ
- ½ cup chopped, cilantro
- Salt and black pepper to taste

Directions:

1. Clean the shrimp. Place in a bowl and add 2 tbsp. oil, black pepper, and salt. Mix gently. Set aside.
2. Make the sauce. Turn on medium - low heat and place a saucepan. Add 1 tbsp. oil. Cook the jalapeno, garlic and onion for 5 minutes. Add the BBQ. Keep warm.
3. Preheat the grill to 450F with closed lid.
4. Place the shrimp directly on the grate and grill and cook 3 minutes on each side.
5. Add the shrimp to the sauce and add the cilantro. Stir gently.
6. Serve and enjoy!

Nutrition: Calories: 230 Proteins: 20g Carbs: 4g Fat: 14g

26.   Tomato Bacon Salad

Preparation time: 10 minutes Cooking Time: 1 hour and 30 minutes Total time: 1 hour and 40 minutes Servings: 6-8

Pellet: Hickory

Ingredients:

- 4 Onions, sweet
- 2 tbsp. Wine vinegar
- 6 Bacon slices
- ½ tsp. Black pepper
- 1 tsp. of Salt
- ½ cup Olive oil
- 1-pint halved cherry Tomatoes
- 2 cups Lettuce, chopped
- 1 Cucumber, sliced
- ½ cup Parmesan cheese shaved
- 1 cup of Croutons

Directions:

1. Preheat the grill to smoke with closed lid.

2. Place the onion on the grate and smoke 30 minutes. Take the onions, wrap each with foil and place them on the grill again.
3. Now increase the heat to 350F. Roast onions for 1 hour. Set aside to cool.
4. While the onions are grilling place the bacon and cook 30 minutes. Set aside to cool. Once cooled, crumble.
5. When the onions cool down, chop.
6. Make the dressing. In a bowl combine black pepper, salt, and wine vinegar. Add oil and whisk slowly.
7. Assemble the salad. In a bowl add the lettuce, bacon, onions, tomatoes, and cucumber. Pour the salad dressing. Toss to coat.
8. Top with Parmesan and croutons. Enjoy!

Nutrition: Calories: 180 Protein: 5g Carbs: 8g Fat: 6g

27.   Crushed Potato Dish

Planning Time: 30 minutes Cooking Time: 45 - an hour
Servings: 8

Pellet: Alder

Ingredients:

- 1 little red onion, daintily cut
- 1 little green ringer pepper, daintily cut
- 1 little red ringer pepper, meagerly cut

- 1 little yellow chime pepper, daintily cut
- 3 cups pureed potatoes
- 8 - 10 bacon cuts
- ¼ cup bacon oil or salted margarine (½ stick)
- ¾ cup sharp cream
- 1 ½ teaspoons grill rub
- 3 cups destroyed sharp cheddar (separated)
- 4 cups hash earthy colored potatoes (frozen)

Directions:

1. Get that bacon cooking over medium warmth in a huge skillet. Cook till overall quite fresh. Focus on 5 minutes on the two sides. Then, at that point put away your bacon. Empty the bacon oil into a glass holder and put away. Utilizing a similar skillet, warm up the spread or bacon oil over medium warmth. At the point when adequately warm, sauté chime peppers and red onions. You're focusing on still somewhat firm. At the point when done, put it all away.

2. Grab a meal dish, ideally one that is 9 by 11 inches. Splash with some nonstick cooking shower, then, at that point spread the pureed potatoes out, covering the whole lower part of the dish. Add the sharp cream to the following layer over the potatoes. At the point when

you're set, season it with a portion of the grill rub. Make another layer with the sautéed veggies over the potatoes, leaving the margarine or oil in the dish.

3. Sprinkle your sharp cheddar—only 1½ of the cups. Then, at that point add the frozen hash earthy colored potatoes. Scoop out the remainder of the bacon oil or spread from the sautéed veggies, everywhere on the hash tans, and afterward finish everything off with some scrumptious, disintegrated bacon bits.

4. Add the remainder of the sharp cheddar (1½ cups) over the entire thing, and afterward utilize some aluminum foil to cover the meal dish. Set up your wood pellet smoker barbecue for aberrant cooking. Preheat to 350°F. Utilize whatever pellets you like.

5. Let the entire thing prepare for 45 - an hour. Preferably, you need the cheddar to bubble.

6. Take it out and let it sit for around 10 minutes.

7. Serve!

Nutrition: Calories: 250 Proteins: 38g Carbs: 4g Fat: 20g

28.   Barbecued Filet Mignon

Planning Time: 10 minutes Cooking Time: 20 minutes Servings: 1

Pellet: Alder

Ingredients:

- Salt
- Pepper
- 3 Filet mignons

Directions:

1. Preheat your barbecue to 450 degrees.
2. Season the steak with a decent measure of salt and pepper to improve its flavor.
3. Place on the barbecue and flip following 5 minutes.
4. Grill the two sides for 5 minutes each.
5. Take it out when it looks cooked and present with your number one side dish.

Nutrition: Calories: 165 Protein: 10g Carbs: 2g Fat: 8g

29.   Nuclear Wild Ox Pieces of Poop

Planning Time: 30 minutes Cooking Time: 1 hour and 30 minutes Servings: 10

Pellet: Alder

Ingredients:

- 8 ounces customary cream cheddar (room temp)
- 10 jalapeno peppers (medium)
- ¾ cup cheddar mix and destroyed Monterey Jack (excessive)
- 1 teaspoon smoked paprika
- 1 teaspoon garlic powder
- ½ teaspoon red pepper pieces (excessive)
- Little Smokies wieners (20)
- 10 bacon strips, meagerly cut and split

Directions:

1. Wash the jalapenos, then, at that point cut them up along the length. Get a spoon, or a paring blade on the off chance that you like and utilize that to take out the seeds and the veins. Spot the scooped-out jalapenos on a veggie barbecuing plate and set it with or without.

2. Get a little bowl and blend the destroyed cheddar, cream cheddar, paprika, cayenne pepper, garlic powder, and red pepper chips. Blend them completely. Get your jalapenos which you've burrowed out, and afterward stuff them with the cream cheddar blend.

3. Get your little Smokies wiener, and afterward put it directly onto every one of the cheddar stuffed jalapenos.

4. Grab a portion of the meagerly cut and split bacon strips and fold them over every one of the stuffed jalapenos and their Wiener. Get a few toothpicks. Use them to keep the bacon pleasantly got to the Frankfurter.

5. Set up your wood pellet smoker barbecue so it's prepared for aberrant cooking. Get it preheated to 250°F. Use Hickory or mixes for your wooden pellets.

6. Put your jalapeno peppers in and smoke them at 250°F for somewhere in the range of an hour and a half to 120 minutes. You need to keep it going until the bacon is quite fresh.

7. Take out the nuclear bison butt nuggets, and afterward let them rest for around 5 minutes. Serve!

Nutrition: Calories: 150 Protein: 10g Carbs: 2g Fat: 6g

30.   Brisket Prepared Beans

Planning Time: 20 minutes Cooking Time: 1 hour and 30 minutes Servings: 10

Pellet: Hickory

Ingredients:

- 1 green chime pepper (medium, diced)
- 1 red chime pepper (medium, diced)
- 1 yellow onion (huge, diced)

- 2 - 6 jalapeno peppers (diced)
- 2 tablespoons olive oil (extra-virgin)
- 3 cups brisket level (cleaved)
- 1 can prepared beans (28 ounces)
- 1 can red kidney beans (1 4ounces, flushed, depleted)
- 1 cup grill sauce
- ½ cup earthy colored sugar (pressed)
- 2 teaspoons mustard (ground)
- 3 cloves of garlic (slashed)
- 1 ½ teaspoon dark pepper
- 1 ½ teaspoon fit Salt

Directions:

1. Put a skillet on the fire, on medium warmth. Warm up your olive oil. Throw in the diced jalapenos, peppers, and onions. Mix every so often for 8 minutes.

2. Grab a 4-quart goulash dish. Presently, in your dish, blend in the pork and beans, kidney beans, heated beans, hacked brisket, cooked peppers and onions, earthy colored sugar, grill sauce, garlic, mustard, Salt, and dark pepper. Set up your wood pellet smoker barbecue so it's prepared for aberrant cooking.

3. Preheat your barbecue to 325°F, utilizing whatever pellets you need. Cook your brisket beans on the

barbecue, for an hour and a half to 120 minutes. Keep it revealed as you cook. At the point when it's prepared, you'll know, on the grounds that the beans will get thicker and will have risen also.

4. Rest the nourishment for 15 minutes, before you at long last proceed onward to step number. Serve!

Nutrition: Calories: 200 Protein: 11g Carbs: 2g Fat: 6g

31.   Twice-Heated Spaghetti Squash

Planning Time: 15 minutes Cooking Time: 60 minutes Servings: 2

Pellet: Hickory

Ingredients:

- 1 spaghetti squash (medium)
- 1 tablespoon olive oil (additional virgin)
- 1 teaspoon salt
- ½ teaspoon pepper

- ½ cup Parmesan cheddar (ground, partitioned)
- ½ cup mozzarella cheddar (destroyed, partitioned)

Directions:

1. Cut the squash along the length fifty-fifty. Ensure you're utilizing a blade that is adequately huge, and sufficiently sharp. Whenever you're done, take out the mash and the seeds from every half with a spoon. Rub the inner parts of every 50% of the squash with some olive oil. At the point when you're finished with that, sprinkle the Salt and pepper.

2. Set up your wood pellet smoker barbecue for aberrant cooking. Preheat your barbecue to 375°F with your favored wood pellets.

3. Put every 50% of the squash on the barbecue. Ensure they're both confronting upwards on the barbecue grates, which ought to be quite hot.

4. Bake for 45 minutes, keeping it on the barbecue until the inward temperature of the squash hits 170°F. You'll realize you're done when you think that it's simple to puncture the squash with a fork. Move the squash to your cutting board. Allow it to stay there for 10 minutes so it's anything but a piece. Turn up the temp on your wood pellet smoker barbecue to 425°F.

5. Use a fork to eliminate the tissue from the squash in strands by raking it to and fro. Do be cautious, since you need the shells to stay unblemished. The strands you rake off should look like spaghetti, in case you're doing it right. Put the spaghetti squash strands in an enormous bowl, and afterward include half of your mozzarella and half of your Parmesan cheeses. Consolidate them by blending.

6. Take the blend, and stuff it into the squash shells. At the point when you're set, sprinkle them with the remainder of the Parmesan and mozzarella cheeses.

7. Optional: You can top these with some bacon bits, on the off chance that you like.

8. Allow the stuffed spaghetti squash shells you've presently stuffed to heat at 435°F for 15 minutes, or anyway long it takes the cheddar to go earthy colored. Serve and appreciate.

Nutrition: Calories: 165 Protein: 10g Carbs: 2g Fat: 8g

32.   Bacon-Wrapped Asparagus

Planning Time: 15 minutes Cooking Time: 25 - 30 minutes Servings: 6

Pellet: Hickory

Ingredients:

- 15 - 20 lances of new asparagus (1 pound)
- Olive oil (additional virgin)
- 5 cuts bacon (meagerly cut)
- 1 teaspoon Salt and pepper (or your favored rub)

Directions:

1. Break off the closures of the asparagus, then, at that point trim everything so they're down to a similar length.
2. Separate the asparagus into groups—3 lances for every pack. Then, at that point spritz them with some olive oil. Utilize a piece of bacon to wrap up each pack. At the point when you're set, delicately dust the wrapped pack with some salt and pepper to taste, or your favored rub. Set up your wood pellet smoker barbecue so that it's prepared for circuitous cooking.
3. Put some fiberglass mats on your meshes. Ensure they're the fiberglass kind. This will hold your asparagus back from stalling out on your barbecue entryways. Preheat your barbecue to 400°F, with whatever pellets you like. You can do this as you prep your asparagus.
4. Grill the wraps for 25 minutes to 30 minutes, tops. The objective is to get your asparagus looking overall quite delicate, and the bacon delightfully fresh.

Nutrition: Calories: 250 Proteins: 43g Carbs: 5g Fat: 23g

33.   Garlic Parmesan Wedges

Planning Time: 15 minutes Cooking Time: 35 minutes Servings: 3

Pellet: Hickory

Ingredients:

- 3 reddish brown potatoes (huge)
- 2 teaspoons of garlic powder
- ¾ teaspoon dark pepper
- 1 ½ teaspoons of Salt
- ¾ cup Parmesan cheddar (ground)
- 3 tablespoons new cilantro (hacked, discretionary. You can supplant this with level leaf parsley)
- ½ cup blue cheddar (per serving, as discretionary plunge. Can be supplanted with farm dressing)

Directions:

1. Use some virus water to clean your potatoes as tenderly as you can with a veggie brush. At the point when done, let them dry. Cut your potatoes along the length down the middle. Cut every half into a third.
2. Get all the additional dampness off your potato by cleaning it all away with a paper towel. On the off chance

that you don't do this, you're not going to have fresh wedges! In a huge bowl, toss in your potato wedges, some olive oil, garlic powder, Salt, garlic, and pepper, and afterward throw them with your hands, gently. You need to ensure the flavors and oil get on each wedge.

3. Place your wedges on a nonstick barbecuing plate, or dish, or relaxed. The single layer kind. Ensure it's at any rate 15 x 12 inches.

4. Set up your wood pellet smoker barbecue so it's prepared for roundabout cooking. Preheat your barbecue to 425°F, with whatever wood pellets you like.

5. Set the barbecuing plate upon your preheated barbecue. Broil the wedges for 15 minutes before you flip them. When you turn them, broil them for an additional 15 minutes, or 20 tops. The outside ought to be a pleasant, firm, brilliant earthy colored.

6. Sprinkle your wedges liberally with the Parmesan cheddar. At the point when you're set, decorate it with some parsley, or cilantro, on the off chance that you like. Serve these terrible young men up with some farm dressing, some blue cheddar, or simply eat them that way!

Nutrition: Calories: 351 Proteins: 33g Carbs: 5g Fat: 20g

34.   Hickory Smoked Moink Ball Sticks

Planning Time: 30 minutes Cooking Time: 1 hour and 15 minutes Servings: 6

Pellet: Hickory

Ingredients:

- ½ pound pork hotdog (ground)
- ½ pound ground meat (80% lean)
- 1 egg (huge)
- ½ cup red onions (minced)
- ½ cup Parmesan cheddar (ground)
- ½ cup Italian breadcrumbs
- ¼ cup parsley (finely hacked)
- ¼ cup milk (entirety)
- 2 garlic cloves (minced) or 1 teaspoon garlic (squashed)
- 1 teaspoon oregano
- ½ teaspoon legitimate salt
- ½ teaspoon dark pepper
- ¼ cup grill sauce
- ½ pound bacon cuts (daintily cut, divided)

Directions:

1. Mix up the ground pork frankfurter, ground hamburger, breadcrumbs, Onion, egg, parsley, Parmesan cheddar, garlic, milk, oregano, Salt, and pepper in a huge bowl. Whatever you do, don't exhaust your meat.

2. Make meatballs of 1½ ounces each. They ought to be about 1½ in width. Put them on your Teflon-covered fiberglass mat. Wrap up every meatball down the middle a cut of your daintily cut bacon. Lance your moink balls, three to a stick.

3. Set up your wood pellet smoker barbecue so that it's overall quite prepared for aberrant cooking. Preheat your barbecue to 225°F, with your hickory wood pellets. Smoke the speared moink balls for 30 minutes.

4. Turn up the temperature to 350°F and keep it that path until the inner temperature of your speared moink balls hits 175°F, which should take around 40 to 45 minutes, worst case scenario. At the point when the bacon gets quite fresh, brush your moink balls with whatever grill sauce you like. In a perfect world, you ought to do this as of now of your cook time.

5. Serve the moink ball sticks while they're hot.

Nutrition: Calories: 250 Proteins: 38g Carbs: 4g Fat: 20g

---

35.   Bacon Cheddar Slider

Planning Time: 30 minutes Cooking Time: 15 minutes Servings: 2

Pellet: Hickory

Ingredients:

- 1 pound ground meat (80% lean)
- 1/2 teaspoon of garlic salt
- 1/2 teaspoon salt
- 1/2 teaspoon of garlic
- 1/2 teaspoon onion
- 1/2 teaspoon dark pepper
- 6 bacon cuts, cut down the middle
- 1/2 Cup mayonnaise
- 2 teaspoons of smooth wasabi (discretionary)
- 6 (1 oz) cut sharp cheddar, cut down the middle (discretionary)
- Cut red Onion
- 1/2 Cup cut legitimate dill pickles
- 12 little breads cut evenly
- Ketchup

Directions:

1. Place ground meat, garlic salt, prepared Salt, garlic powder, onion powder and dark hupe pepper in a medium bowl. Separation the meat combination into 12 equivalent parts, shape into little dainty round patties (around 2 ounces each) and save. Cook the bacon on medium warmth over medium warmth for 5-8 minutes until crunchy. Put away. To make the sauce, blend the mayonnaise and horseradish in a little bowl, whenever utilized. Preheat wood pellet smoker barbecue to 350°F utilizing chosen pellets. Iron surface ought to be around 400°F.

2. Spray a cooking shower on the iron cooking surface for best non-stick results. Barbecue the clay for 3-4 minutes each until the interior temperature arrives at 160°F.

3. If fundamental, place a sharp cheddar cut on every patty while the patty is on the iron or after the patty is taken out from the frying pan.

4. Place a limited quantity of mayonnaise combination, a cut of red Onion, and a cheeseburger pate in the lower half of each roll. Cured cuts, bacon and ketchup.

Nutrition: Calories: 400 Proteins: 36g Carbs: 4g Fat: 20g

36. Mushrooms Loaded Down with Crab Meat

Planning Time: 20 minutes Cooking Time: 30 – 45 minutes Servings: 6

Pellet: Apple

Ingredients:

- 6 medium-sized portobello mushrooms
- Additional virgin olive oil
- 1/3 Ground parmesan cheddar cup

club beat staffing:

- 8 oz new crab meat or canned or impersonation crab meat
- 2 tablespoons additional virgin olive oil
- 1/3 Cleaved celery
- Cleaved red peppers
- 1/2 cup cleaved green onion
- 1/2 cup Italian breadcrumbs
- 1/2 Cup mayonnaise
- 8 oz cream cheddar at room temperature
- 1/2 teaspoon of garlic
- 1 tablespoon dried parsley
- Ground parmesan cheddar cup
- 1 teaspoon of Old Inlet preparing
- 1/4 teaspoon of genuine Salt
- 1/4 teaspoon dark pepper

Directions:

1. Clean the mushroom cap with a sodden paper towel. Remove the stem and save it. Eliminate the earthy colored gills from the lower part of the mushroom cap with a spoon and dispose of.

2. Prepare crab meat stuffing. If you are utilizing canned crab meat, channel, flush, and eliminate shellfish. Warmth the olive oil in a griddle over medium high warmth. Add celery, peppers and green onions and fry for 5 minutes. Put away for cooling. Tenderly pour the chilled sautéed vegetables and the leftover fixings into an enormous bowl. Cover and refrigerate crab meat stuffing until prepared to utilize.

3. Put the crab blend in each mushroom cap and make a hill in the middle.

4. Sprinkle additional virgin olive oil and sprinkle parmesan cheddar on each stuffed mushroom cap. Put the mushrooms in a 10 x 15-inch heating dish. Utilize the pellets to set the wood pellet smoker barbecue to aberrant warming and preheat to 375°F.

5. Bake for 30-45 minutes until the filling gets hot (165°F as estimated by a moment read computerized thermometer) and the mushrooms start to deliver juice.

Nutrition: Calories: 250 Proteins: 38g Carbs: 4g Fat: 0g

37. Parmesan Tomatoes

Planning Time: 110 minutes Cooking Time: 20 minutes Servings: 6

Pellet: Apple

Ingredients:

- 9 divided Tomatoes
- 1 cup ground Parmesan cheddar
- 1/2 teaspoon Ground dark pepper
- 1/4 teaspoon Onion powder
- 1 tablespoon Dried rosemary

- 2 tablespoons. Olive oil
- 5 minced Garlic cloves
- 1 teaspoon Legitimate Salt

Directions:

1. Heat a barbecue to medium-low warmth and oil grates. Spot tomatoes parts cut side down, onto the barbecue and cook for 5-7 minutes.
2. Heat olive oil in a container over a medium warmth. Add garlic, rosemary, dark pepper, onion powder, and Salt and cook for 3-5 minutes.
3. Remove from warmth and put away. Flip every tomato half and brush with olive oil garlic blend and top with ground parmesan cheddar. Close barbecue and cook for 7-10 minutes more until cheddar is liquefied.
4. Remove tomatoes from the barbecue and serve right away.

Nutrition: Calories: 260 Proteins: 28g Carbs: 4g Fat: 20g

38. Feta Spinach Turkey Burgers

Planning Time: 10 minutes Cooking Time: 10 minutes Servings: 4

Pellet: Alder

Ingredients:

- 1 lb. Ground turkey
- 1 tablespoon Breadcrumbs
- 1/4 teaspoon Squashed red pepper
- 1 teaspoon Parsley

- 1 teaspoon Oregano
- 1 teaspoon Garlic powder
- 1/3 cup. Sun-dried tomatoes
- 1/2 cup, disintegrated Feta cheddar
- 1/2 cup, slashed Child spinach
- 1/2 teaspoon Pepper
- 1/2 teaspoon Ocean salt

Directions:

1. Add all fixings into the blending bowl and blend until just joined. Make four equivalent formed patties from the blend. Preheat the barbecue to high warmth.
2. Place patties on a hot barbecue and cook for 3-5 minutes on each side or until inner temperature compasses to 165°F. Serve

Nutrition: Calories: 250 Proteins: 38g Carbs: 4g Fat: 20g

39. Curried Cauliflower Sticks

Planning Time: 15 minutes Cooking Time: 15 minutes Servings: 6

Pellet: Alder

Ingredients:

- 1 cut into florets enormous cauliflower head
- 1 cut into wedges onion
- 1 cut into squares yellow chime pepper
- 1 new lemon juice
- 1/4 cup olive oil

- 1/2 teaspoon garlic powder
- 1/2 teaspoon ground ginger
- 3 teaspoons curry powder
- 1/2 teaspoon salt

Directions:

1. In an enormous blending bowl, whisk together oil, lemon juice, garlic, ginger, curry powder, and Salt. Add cauliflower florets and throw until very much covered. Warmth the barbecue to medium warmth.
2. Thread cauliflower florets, Onion, and ringer pepper onto the sticks.
3. Place sticks onto the hot barbecue and cook for 6-7 minutes on each side. Serve.

Nutrition: Calories: 180 Protein: 5g Carbs: 2g Fat: 8g

40. Southwest Chicken Drumsticks

Planning Time: 10 minutes Cooking Time: 30 minutes Servings: 8

Pellet: Alder

Ingredients:

- 2 lbs. Chicken legs
- 2 tablespoons. Taco preparing

- 2 tablespoons. Olive oil

Directions:

1. Preheat the barbecue to a medium-high warmth and oil grates. Brush chicken legs with oil and rub with taco preparing.
2. Place chicken legs on the hot barbecue and cook for 30 minutes. Turn chicken legs after like clockwork. Serve.

Nutrition: Calories: 170 Protein: 5g Carbs: 2g Fat: 8g

41. Yam Fries

Planning Time: 10 minutes Cooking Time: 12 minutes Servings: 4

Pellet: Cherry

Ingredients:

- 2 lbs. stripped and cut into ½-inch wedges Yams
- 2 tablespoons. Olive oil
- Pepper and Salt to taste

Directions:

1. Preheat the barbecue to medium-high warmth. Throw yams with oil, pepper, and Salt.
2. Place yam wedges on a hot barbecue and cook over a medium warmth for 6 minutes. Flip and cook for 6-8 minutes more.
3. Serve.

Nutrition: Calories: 80 Protein: 50g Carbs: 5g Fat: 10g

42. Smoked Cashews

Planning Time: 5 minutes Cooking Time: 1-hour Servings: 4 to 6

Pellet: Cherry

Ingredients:

- 1 pound (454 g) broiled, salted cashews

Directions:

1. Supply your smoker with wood pellets and follow the producer's particular beginning up strategy. Preheat the barbecue, with the cover shut, to 120°F (49°C).
2. Pour the cashews onto a rimmed heating sheet and smoke for 60 minutes, mixing once part of the way through the smoking time.
3. Remove the cashews from the barbecue, let cool, and store in a water/air proof compartment however long you can stand up to.

Nutrition: Calories: 180 Protein: 5g Carbs: 2g Fat: 8g

43. Simple Eggs

Planning Time: 10 minutes Cooking Time: 30 minutes Servings: 12

Pellet: Cherry

Ingredients:

- 12 hardboiled eggs, stripped and flushed

Directions:

1. Supply your smoker with wood pellets and follow the producer's particular beginning up methodology. Preheat the barbecue, with the top shut, to 120°F (49°C).
2. Place the eggs straightforwardly on the barbecue mesh and smoke for 30 minutes. They will start to take on a slight earthy colored sheen. Eliminate the eggs and refrigerate for in any event 30 minutes prior to serving. Refrigerate any extras in a hermetically sealed holder for 1 or fourteen days

Nutrition: Calories: 167 Protein: 7g Carbs: 3g Fat: 8g

44. Cheddar with Saltines

Planning Time: 5 minutes Cooking Time: 2½ hours Servings: 4

Pellet: Hickory

Ingredients:

- 1 (2-pounds/907-g) block medium cheddar, or your #1 cheddar, quartered longwise

Directions:

1. Supply your smoker with wood pellets and follow the maker's particular beginning up method. Preheat the barbecue, with the top shut, to 90°F (32°C).

2. Place the cheddar straightforwardly on the barbecue mesh and smoke for 2 hours, 30 minutes, checking as often as possible to be certain it's anything but dissolving. On the off chance that the cheddar starts to dissolve, have a go at flipping it. If that doesn't help, eliminate it from the barbecue and refrigerate for around 1 hour and afterward return it to the chilly smoker.
3. Remove the cheddar, place it's anything but a zip-top pack, and refrigerate for the time being.
4. Slice the cheddar and present with wafers or mesh it and use for making a smoked Macintosh and cheddar.

Nutrition: Calories: 180 Protein: 5g Carbs: 2g Fat: 8g

45. Bacon and Crab Cheddar Poppers

Planning Time: 20 minutes Cooking Time: 30 to 40 minutes Servings 6 to 8

Pellet: Hickory

Ingredients:

- 12 enormous jalapeño peppers
- 8 ounces (227 g) cream cheddar, at room temperature
- Finely ground zing of 1 lemon
- 1 teaspoon Old Narrows preparing, or to taste
- 8 ounces (227 g) crab meat, depleted, picked over, and finely destroyed or hacked
- Sweet or smoked paprika, for sprinkling
- 12 strips distinctive bacon, cut across down the middle

Directions:

1. Set up your smoker adhering to the maker's guidelines and preheat to 350°F (177°C). (Indeed, I realize this is more sizzling than the traditional low and moderate strategy—it gives you crisper bacon.) Add the wood as indicated by the producer.

2. Cut each jalapeño fifty-fifty the long way, slicing through the stem and leaving it set up. Scratch out the seeds and veins; a grapefruit spoon or melon hotshot functions admirably for this. Organize the jalapeño parts on a wire rack, cut side up.

3. Place the cream cheddar in a blending bowl. Add the lemon zing and Old Straight flavoring and beat with a wooden spoon until light. Tenderly crease in the crab. Spoon a stacking tablespoon of crab combination into each jalapeño half, mounding it toward the middle. Sprinkle with paprika. Wrap each jalapeño half with a piece of bacon (you need the filling uncovered at each end). Secure the bacon with a toothpick and organize the poppers in a solitary layer on the wire rack.

4. Place the wire rack in the smoker. Smoke the poppers until the bacon and filling are cooked and the peppers are delicate (crush them between your thumb and pointer), 30 to 40 minutes.

5. Transfer the poppers to a platter. Let cool marginally prior to serving.

Nutrition: Calories: 180 Protein: 5g Carbs: 2g Fat: 8g

46. Tomato and Cucumber Gazpacho

Planning Time: 30 minutes Cooking Time: 1-hour Servings 4

Pellet: Hickory

Ingredients:

- 4 tasty red ready tomatoes (around 2 pounds/907 g), cut down the middle widthwise
- 1 medium-size cucumber, stripped, cut down the middle longwise, seeds scratched out

- ½ green or yellow ringer pepper, stemmed, cultivated, and cut into 2 pieces
- ½ red ringer pepper, stemmed, cultivated, and cut into 2 pieces
- 1 little sweet onion, stripped and cut longwise in quarters
- 1 clove garlic, stripped
- 3 tablespoons great additional virgin olive oil, in addition to extra for showering
- Around 2 tablespoons red wine or Spanish sherry vinegar
- ½ cup water, in addition to extra on a case-by-case basis
- Coarse salt (ocean or genuine) and newly ground dark pepper, to taste
- 1 tablespoon slashed new chives or scallion greens

Directions:

1. Arrange the tomatoes, cucumber, peppers, and onion, cut side up, in an aluminum foil skillet. Add the garlic. Set up your smoker for cold smoking, adhering to the producer's guidelines. Add the wood as determined by the maker.
2. Place the vegetables in the smoker. Smoke until tanned with smoke (plunge your finger in one cut tomato—the

juices should taste smoky), 60 minutes, or depending on the situation. The vegetables ought to stay crude.

3. Cut the vegetables into 1-inch pieces, holding the juices. Spot in a food processor and interaction to a coarse or smooth puree (your decision). Continuously add the saved juices, oil, vinegar, and enough water (about ½ cup) to make a pourable soup. Work in salt and pepper to taste, in addition to a couple of more drops of vinegar if necessary, to adjust the pleasantness of the vegetables. Then again, place the vegetables and their juices, oil, vinegar, and water in a blender and mix to your favored consistency. Season with salt, pepper, and more vinegar. The gazpacho can be made a few hours ahead to this stage, covered, and refrigerated, yet taste and re-season it prior to serving.

4. Ladle the gazpacho into serving bowls. Shower extra olive oil on top and sprinkle with the cleaved chives.

Nutrition: Calories: 180 Protein: 5g Carbs: 2g Fat: 8g

47. Chicken Livers with White Wine

Planning Time: 15 minutes Cooking Time: 30 to 40 minutes
Servings 4

Pellet: Hickory

Ingredients.

- 1 pound (454 g) chicken or turkey livers
- 1 cup heated water
- 1½ tablespoons coarse salt (ocean or legitimate)
- 1 teaspoon dark peppercorns
- ½ teaspoon new or dried thyme leaves
- 1 cup ice water
- ½ cup dry white wine
- Vegetable oil, for oiling the rack
- Around 1 tablespoon additional virgin olive oil
- 1 tablespoon spread or bacon fat, for searing (discretionary)

Directions:

1. Trim any green or ridiculous spots off the livers.
2. Make the saline solution: Spot the high temp water, salt, peppercorns, and thyme in a profound bowl and rush

until the salt disintegrates. Race in the ice water and wine. At the point when the combination is cold, mix in the chicken livers. Brackish water, covered, in the cooler for 3 hours.

3. Drain the livers in a colander and smear dry with paper towels. Oil a wire rack and organize the livers on it. Give dry access the fridge for 30 minutes. Daintily brush the livers with olive oil on the two sides.

4. Meanwhile, set up your smoker adhering to the producer's directions and preheat to 300°F (149°C). Add the wood as determined by the producer. Spot the rack in the smoker and smoke the livers until cooked to taste, 30 to 40 minutes for pink in the middle. (Make a cut in one of the livers to check for doneness.) Don't overcook.

5. You can serve the livers hot from the smoker. To add a little smash to the outside, soften the spread in an enormous skillet over high warmth. Sauté the livers until singed and dry, 1 to 2 minutes for each side.

48. Chicken and Bean Cheddar Nachos

Planning Time: 20 minutes Cooking Time: 12 to 15 minutes Servings 6 to 8

Pellet: Hickory

Ingredients:

- 8 cups tortilla chips
- 2 cups destroyed smoked brisket or chicken
- 1 can (15 ounces/425 g) dark beans (ideally natural and low sodium), depleted well in a colander, washed, and depleted once more
- 12 ounces (340 g) finely ground blended cheeses (like Cheddar, smoked Cheddar, Jack, or potentially pepper Jack; around 3 cups)
- 4 new jalapeño peppers, stemmed and meagerly cut across, or ⅓ cup depleted cured jalapeño cuts
- 4 scallions, managed, white and green parts daintily cut across
- 2 to 4 tablespoons of your number one hot sauce (I like Cholula) or grill sauce
- ¼ cup coarsely slashed new cilantro (discretionary)

Directions:

1. Set up your smoker adhering to the producer's directions and preheat to 275°F (135°C). Add the wood as determined by the producer.

2. Loosely orchestrate 33% of the tortilla contributes the barbecue skillet. Sprinkle 33% of the destroyed brisket, beans, cheddar, jalapeños, and scallions on top. Shake on hot sauce. Add a second layer of these fixings, trailed by a third. Spot the skillet with the nachos in your smoker and smoke until the cheddar is liquefied and gurgling, 12 to 15 minutes.

3. Sprinkle the cilantro on top, if utilizing, and dive in. Indeed—you eat the nachos directly out of the skillet, so be mindful so as not to consume your fingers on the edge.

4. Smoked Nachos on the Barbecue

5. Set up the barbecue for circuitous barbecuing and preheat to medium-high 400°F (204°C). Spot the nachos container on the mesh away from the warmth and throw the wood chips on the coals. Roundabout barbecue until the cheddar is softened and percolating, 5 minutes.

Nutrition: Calories: 200 Protein: 8g Carbs: 2g Fat: 3g

49. Margarine Chicken Wings with Peanuts

Planning Time: 15 minutes Cooking Time: ½ to 2 hours Servings 4 to 6

Pellet: Apple

Ingredients:

- 3 pounds (1.4 kg) chicken wings (around 24 pieces)
- ½ cup finely slashed new cilantro
- 2 teaspoons coarse salt (ocean or fit)

- 2 teaspoons broke dark peppercorns
- 2 teaspoons ground coriander (discretionary)
- 2 tablespoons Asian (dull) sesame oil
- Vegetable oil, for oiling the rack
- 6 tablespoons (¾ stick) spread
- 4 jalapeño peppers, daintily cut across (leave the seeds in)
- 6 tablespoons sriracha (or other most loved hot sauce)
- ¼ cup cleaved dry-broiled peanuts

Directions:

1. Place the chicken wings in an enormous bowl. Sprinkle in ¼ cup of the cilantro, the salt, pepper, and coriander, if utilizing, and mix to blend. Mix in the sesame oil. Cover the bowl and marinate, refrigerated, for 15 to an hour (the more they marinate, the more extravagant the flavor).

2. Meanwhile, set up your smoker adhering to the maker's directions and preheat to 375°F (191°C). (In the event that your smoker's unequipped for arriving at that temperature, preheat as hot as the smoker will go.) Add the wood as determined by the maker. Oil the smoker rack and organize the drumettes on it. Smoke the wings until sizzling, earthy colored with smoke, and cooked

through, 30 to 50 minutes. At lower temperatures, for instance, at 250°F (121°C), you'll need 1½ to 2 hours. In certain smokers, the pieces nearest to the fire will cook quicker; if so, pivot the pieces so all cook uniformly. To check for doneness, make a little cut in the thickest piece of a couple of the wings. The meat at the bone ought to be white, without any hints of red. Try not to overcook. Orchestrate the wings on a heatproof platter.

3. Just prior to serving, liquefy the spread in a cast-iron skillet on the oven over high warmth. Add the jalapeños and cook until they sizzle and begin to brown, 3 minutes. Mix in the sriracha and heat to the point of boiling. Pour over the chicken.

4. Sprinkle the chicken with the peanuts and the excess ¼ cup cilantro and serve immediately with a lot of napkins.

Nutrition: Calories: 260 Protein: 5g Carbs: 2g Fat: 8g

50. Nectar Bread

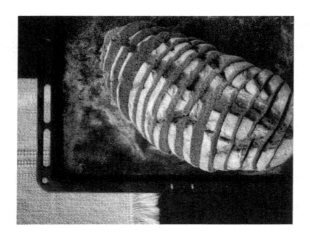

Planning Time: 10 minutes Cooking Time: 1½ to 2 hours
Servings 1 portion

Pellet: Apple

Ingredients:

- 2 cups unbleached universally handy white flour or on a case-by-case basis
- 1 cup entire wheat flour or 1 extra cup white flour
- 1 teaspoon coarse salt (ocean or legitimate), in addition to extra for sprinkling

- 1¼ cups water, in addition to extra on a case-by-case basis
- 1 envelope (2½ teaspoons) dry yeast
- 2 tablespoons nectar
- 1 tablespoon additional virgin olive oil, in addition to oil for the bowl, portion dish, and top of the bread

Directions:

1. Set up your smoker adhering to the producer's guidelines and preheat it as low as it will go (200°F (93°C) or underneath). Spread out the flours and salt in a far layer (not more than ¼ inch thick) in an aluminum foil skillet or on a rimmed preparing sheet. Spot the water in another foil dish.

2. Place the container in the smoker and smoke until the white flour is delicately sautéed on a superficial level and tastes smoky and the water tastes smoky. All out smoking time is 15 to 20 minutes for hot-smoking or 1 to 1½ hours for cold-smoking.

3. Let the flours cool to room temperature. The water should simply cool to warm 105°F (41°C).

4. Place the smoked flours, smoked salt, and yeast in a food processor and cycle to blend. Add the nectar, olive oil, and the smoked warm water. Interaction in short blasts to acquire a delicate, malleable mixture. On the off

chance that the batter is excessively solid, add somewhat warmer faucet water; if excessively delicate, add somewhat more flour. Then again, you can blend and work the batter by hand or in a stand blender fitted with a mixture snare. Turn the batter onto a daintily floured cutting board and ply by hand into a smooth ball.

5. Place the batter in a huge delicately oiled bowl, going it to oil the two sides. Cover with cling wrap and let the batter ascend in a warm spot until multiplied in mass, 1 to 1½ hours.

6. Punch down the batter, work it's anything but an oval shape, and spot it's anything but an oiled portion skillet. Cover with saran wrap. Allow the mixture to rise again until multiplied in mass, 30 minutes to 60 minutes.

7. Meanwhile, set up a barbecue for backhanded barbecuing and preheat to 400°F (204°C) or preheat your stove to 400°F (204°C). On the off chance that your smoker goes up to 400°F (204°C), you can prepare the bread in it. No compelling reason to add wood—you've effectively smoked the flour.

Nutrition: Calories: 380 Protein: 5g Carbs: 8g Fat: 7g

51. Bacon and Crab Cheddar Poppers

Planning Time: 20 minutes Cooking Time: 30 to 40 minutes Servings 6 to 8

Pellet: Alder

Ingredients:

- 2 enormous jalapeño peppers
- 8 ounces (227 g) cream cheddar, at room temperature
- Finely ground zing of 1 lemon
- 1 teaspoon Old Narrows preparing, or to taste
- 8 ounces (227 g) crab meat, depleted, picked over, and finely destroyed or hacked
- Sweet or smoked paprika, for sprinkling
- 12 strips distinctive bacon, cut across down the middle

Directions:

1. Set up your smoker adhering to the maker's guidelines and preheat to 350°F (177°C). (Indeed, I realize this is more sizzling than the traditional low and moderate strategy—it gives you crisper bacon.) Add the wood as indicated by the producer.

2. Cut each jalapeño fifty-fifty the long way, slicing through the stem and leaving it set up. Scratch out the seeds and veins; a grapefruit spoon or melon hotshot functions admirably for this. Organize the jalapeño parts on a wire rack, cut side up.

3. Place the cream cheddar in a blending bowl. Add the lemon zing and Old Straight flavoring and beat with a wooden spoon until light. Tenderly crease in the crab. Spoon a stacking tablespoon of crab combination into each jalapeño half, mounding it toward the middle. Sprinkle with paprika. Wrap each jalapeño half with a piece of bacon (you need the filling uncovered at each end). Secure the bacon with a toothpick and organize the poppers in a solitary layer on the wire rack.

4. Place the wire rack in the smoker. Smoke the poppers until the bacon and filling are cooked and the peppers are delicate (crush them between your thumb and pointer), 30 to 40 minutes.

5. Transfer the poppers to a platter. Let cool marginally prior to serving.

Nutrition: Calories: 215 Protein: 6g Carbs: 21g Fat: 6g

52. Smoked Cashews

Planning Time: 5 minutes Cooking Time: 1-hour Servings: 4 to 6

Pellet: Pecan

Ingredients:

- 1 pound (454 g) broiled, salted cashews

Directions:

1. Supply your smoker with wood pellets and follow the producer's particular beginning up strategy. Preheat the barbecue, with the cover shut, to 120°F (49°C).
2. Pour the cashews onto a rimmed heating sheet and smoke for 60 minutes, mixing once part of the way through the smoking time.
3. Remove the cashews from the barbecue, let cool, and store in a water/air proof compartment however long you can stand up to.

Nutrition: Calories: 215 Protein: 6g Carbs: 21g Fat: 6g

53. Simple Eggs

Planning Time: 10 minutes Cooking Time: 30 minutes Servings: 12

Pellet: Pecan

Ingredients:

- 12 hardboiled eggs, stripped and flushed

Directions:

1. Supply your smoker with wood pellets and follow the producer's particular beginning up methodology. Preheat the barbecue, with the top shut, to 120°F (49°C).
2. Place the eggs straightforwardly on the barbecue mesh and smoke for 30 minutes. They will start to take on a slight earthy colored sheen. Eliminate the eggs and refrigerate for in any event 30 minutes prior to serving. Refrigerate any extras in a hermetically sealed holder for 1 or fourteen days

Nutrition: Calories: 215 Protein: 6g Carbs: 21g Fat: 6g

54. Onion with Bacon and Cheddar

Planning time: 20 minutes Cooking time: 2½ to 3 hours Servings 4 onions

Pellet: Alder

Ingredients:

- 4 huge (12-to 14-ounces/340-to 397-g every) sweet onions, stripped
- 3 tablespoons unsalted spread
- 4 strips distinctive bacon cut across into ¼-inch fragments
- 4 jalapeño peppers, cultivated and diced (for spicier onions, leave the seeds in)
- ½ cup grill sauce (utilize your top pick)
- ½ cup ground Cheddar or pepper Jack cheddar (discretionary)

Directions:

1. Using a sharp paring blade and beginning at the top (inverse the root), cut an altered cone-molded pit around 2 creeps across the top and 2 inches somewhere down in every onion. (The center should turn out in a cone-molded attachment.) Hack the pieces you eliminate.

2. Melt 1 tablespoon of the margarine in a medium-size skillet. Add the hacked onion, bacon, and jalapeños and cook over medium warmth, blending every so often, until softly caramelized, 4 minutes. Spot a spoonful of the filling in the depression of every onion. Gap the leftover 2 tablespoons of margarine into 4 taps and spot one on top of every onion. (The onions can be arranged a few hours ahead to this stage. Spot them on a plate, cover with cling wrap, and refrigerate.)

3. Set up your smoker adhering to the producer's guidelines and preheat to 225°F (107°C) to 250°F (121°C). Add the wood as indicated by the maker.

4. Place the onions on barbecue rings or in a shallow aluminum foil container. Smoke until delicately yielding when crushed on the sides, around 2 hours.

5. Place 2 tablespoons of the grill sauce on every onion and top with 2 tablespoons of the cheddar, if utilizing. Keep smoking the onions for another 30 to an hour. To test for doneness, crush the sides of the onion—they ought to be delicate and simple to puncture with a metal stick. Move the onions to a platter or plates for serving.

Nutrition: Calories: 35g Protein: 5.5g Carbs: 5g Fat: 2g

CPSIA information can be obtained
at www.ICGtesting.com
Printed in the USA
BVHW052124030821
613540BV00009B/264